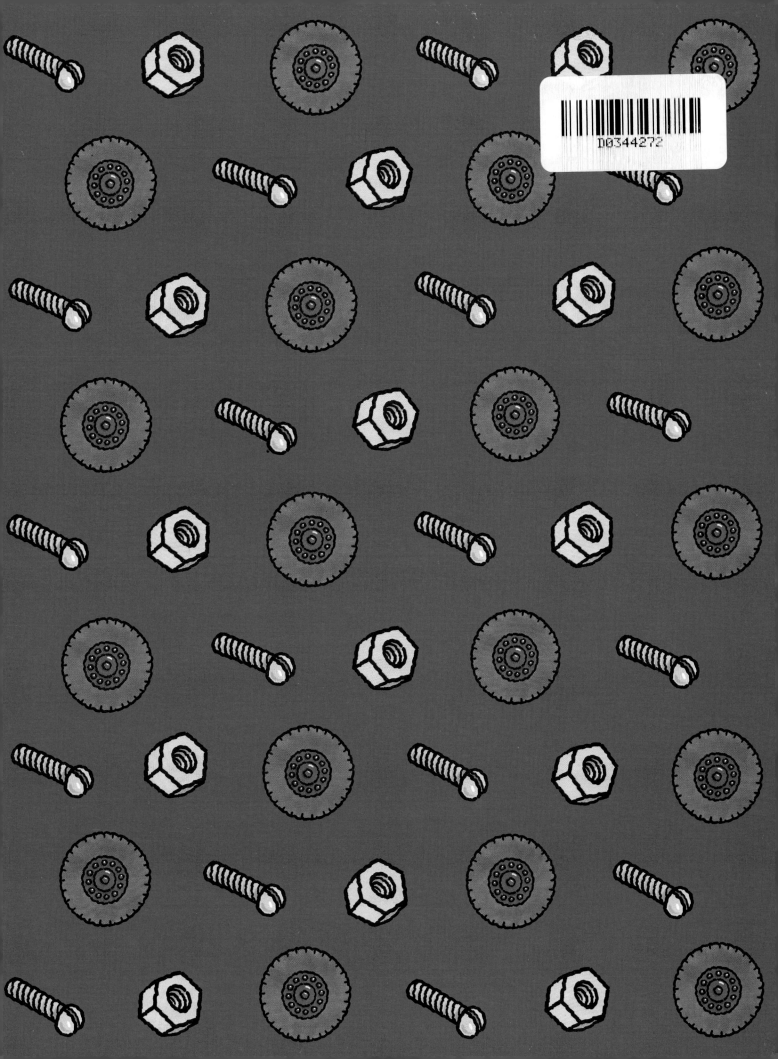

A DORLING KINDERSLEY BOOK

Editor Lara Tankel
Senior Editor Mary Ling
Designer Helen Melville
Additional Design Mike Buckley
Managing Editor Sheila Hanly
Production Josie Alabaster
Photography Lynton Gardiner
Illustrator Derek Matthews
Consultant 1st Officer Louise Lipman

First published in Great Britain in 1995
by Dorling Kindersley Limited,
9 Henrietta Street, London WC2E 8PS

A CIP catalogue record for this book
is available from the British Library.

ISBN: 0-7513-53094

Colour reproduction by Chromagraphics, Singapore
Printed and bound in Italy by L.E.G.O.

The publisher would like to thank the following for
their kind permission to reproduce their photographs:
t=top, b=bottom, c=centre, l=left, r=right
Robert Harding Picture Library 7t;/Ian Griffiths 5b, 11t;
Quadrant Picture Library/Flight 17c;/McBain 4tl;
Pictures Colour Library 6/7c;
Tony Stone Images 17b/Mark Wagner 17t.

Every effort has been made to trace the copyright holders
and we apologise in advance for any unintentional
omissions. We would be pleased to insert the appropriate
acknowledgment in any subsequent edition
of this publication.

Scale

Look out for drawings like
this – they show the size of
the machines compared
with people.

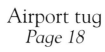

Mighty Machines

AEROPLANE

Christopher Maynard

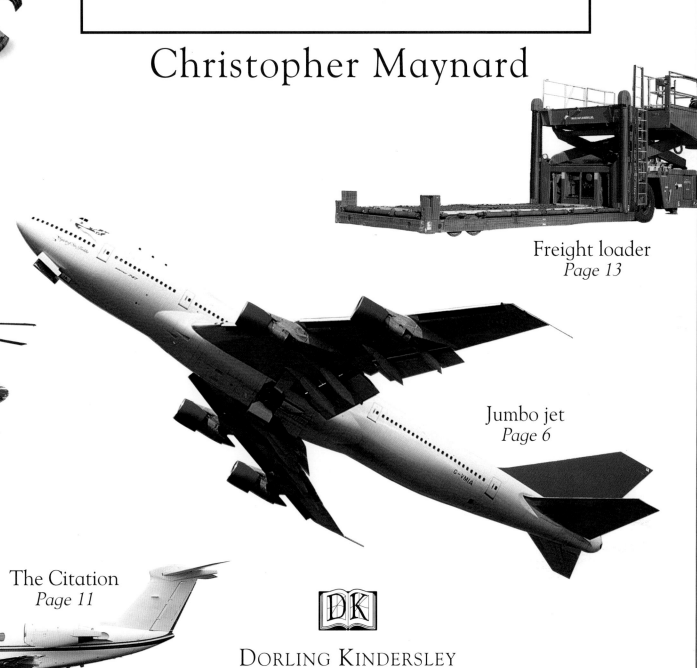

Freight loader
Page 13

Jumbo jet
Page 6

The Citation
Page 11

DORLING KINDERSLEY
LONDON • NEW YORK • STUTTGART

Jumbo jet

Cabin air is so dry that sliced bread turns hard in a few minutes.

The 747 "jumbo jet" is the biggest airliner in the world. It can carry over 400 passengers and crew in its cabin. It has four huge jet engines to push it along. It flies best at a height of about 10,500 m – that's 20 times higher than the tallest skyscraper.

cabin windows

body of the plane is called the fuselage

The jumbo is 64 m wide between wing tips – the width of 35 family cars parked side by side.

Painting an airline's colours on a 747 adds up to the weight of a big horse.

Jumbos travel at 930 kph – 100 times faster than you cycle.

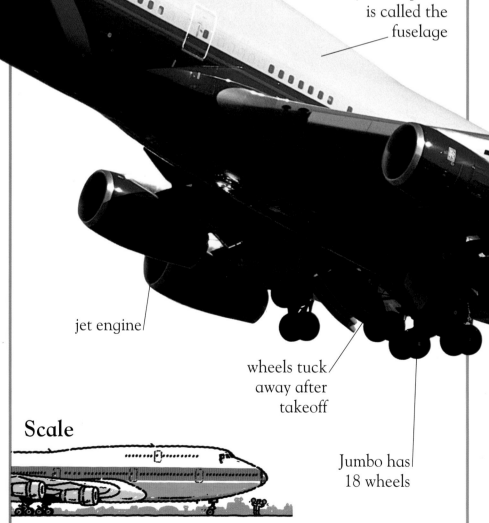

jet engine

wheels tuck away after takeoff

Jumbo has 18 wheels

Scale

In **jet** planes, hot gases rush out of the back of the engines to push the plane along.

Firing range

The windows of a 747 are as thick as your fist. They are made of two pieces of glass with plastic in between. To test their strength small objects are fired very quickly at the front windows.

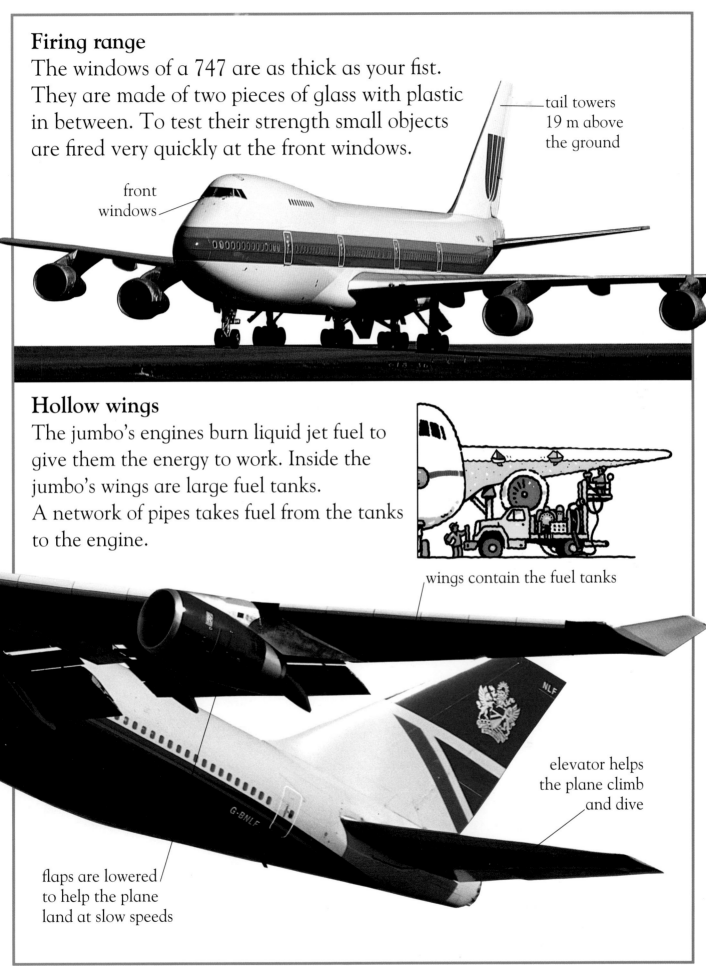

tail towers 19 m above the ground

front windows

Hollow wings

The jumbo's engines burn liquid jet fuel to give them the energy to work. Inside the jumbo's wings are large fuel tanks. A network of pipes takes fuel from the tanks to the engine.

wings contain the fuel tanks

elevator helps the plane climb and dive

flaps are lowered to help the plane land at slow speeds

A tail is fixed to the **fuselage** to stop the plane swinging from side to side.

Fuel tanker

⬡ In just one minute, a pumper truck could fill up the tanks of 32 estate cars.

⬡ It takes 204,350 litres of fuel to fill a 747. This would fill a big swimming pool.

Aircraft must be filled up with jet fuel before they can take off. The fuel tanker drives about an airport, carrying thousands of litres of fuel. It stops by waiting planes and pumps fuel into their wing tanks through a thick hose.

Scale

pump can deliver 2,300 litres of fuel every minute

Hutchinson

T46

T46

1863 JET A

FLAMMABLE

tanker body is full of jet fuel

A **pump** forces liquid, such as fuel, from one place to another.

Pump it up

Major airports have large reservoirs full of fuel. Underground pipes carry the fuel near to the planes. Pumper trucks then pump fuel from the pipes into the planes through their hoses.

rear platform rises so hose can reach the high wings of a jet

hose

driver's cab can be unhooked from the main tanker

beacon

driver has a clear view all around

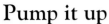 A **reservoir** is a place where liquids are collected and stored for use.

Small planes

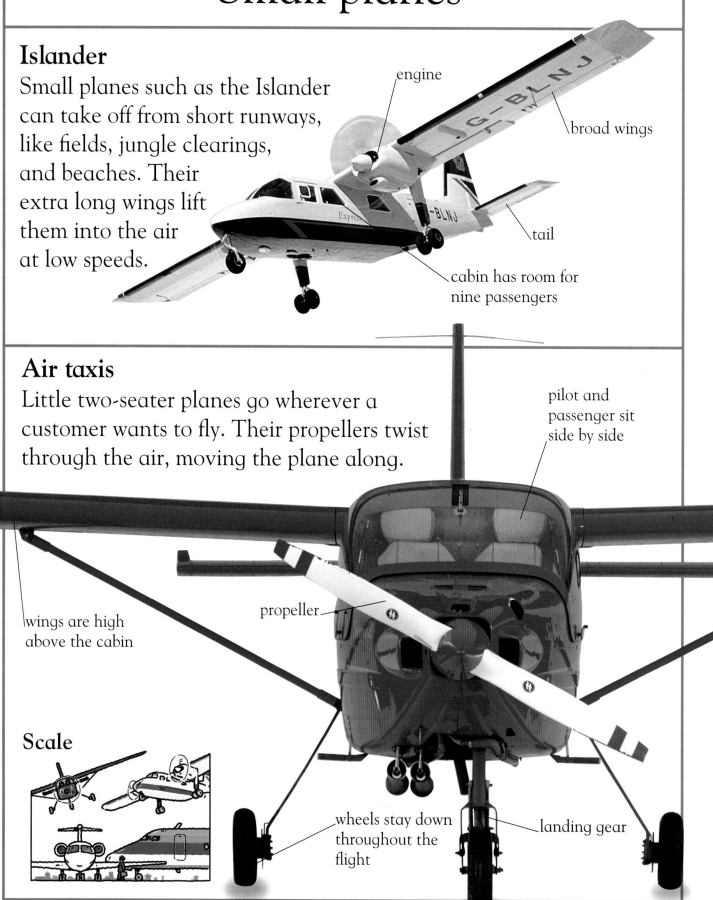

Islander

Small planes such as the Islander can take off from short runways, like fields, jungle clearings, and beaches. Their extra long wings lift them into the air at low speeds.

engine

broad wings

tail

cabin has room for nine passengers

Air taxis

Little two-seater planes go wherever a customer wants to fly. Their propellers twist through the air, moving the plane along.

pilot and passenger sit side by side

wings are high above the cabin

propeller

Scale

wheels stay down throughout the flight

landing gear

The **landing gear** lets the aircraft move safely and smoothly on the ground.

AMAZING FACTS

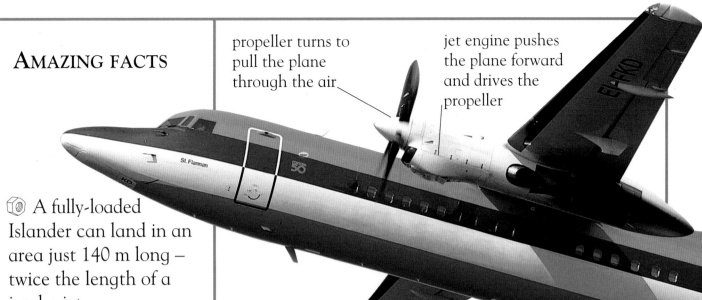

propeller turns to pull the plane through the air

jet engine pushes the plane forward and drives the propeller

🔩 A fully-loaded Islander can land in an area just 140 m long – twice the length of a jumbo jet.

🔩 Business jets carry folding air stairs. These flip down when the door opens, so passengers can reach the ground.

Fokker 50

This busy 50-seater plane is driven by "turboprops", which means it is powered by propellers and jet engines. It flies at a height of 7,600 m between England and Ireland, four times a day.

long, thin wings give plenty of lift

The Citation

The Citation is a business jet. It is owned by a company whose workers need to travel. It can fly seven workers at speeds of up to 790 kph – not much slower than a jumbo jet.

passenger cabin barely wider than a car

jet engine at the back

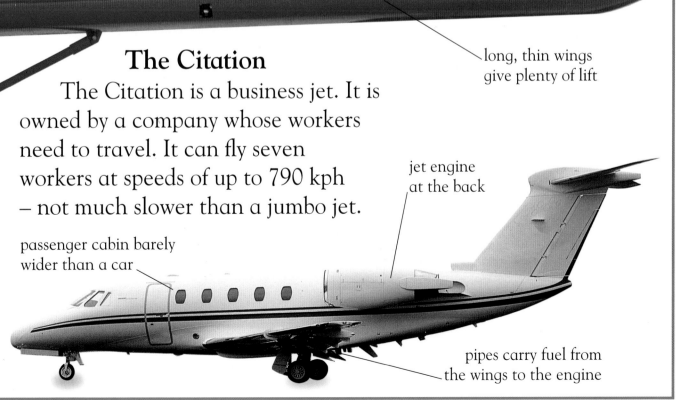

pipes carry fuel from the wings to the engine

🔩 Air flowing over a plane's curved wings creates a force called **lift** to pull it up. 🔩

Plane loaders

An airbridge is a vehicle with an electric engine. It moves to fit between the passenger building, or terminal, and aircraft door. People then walk through it on to their plane.

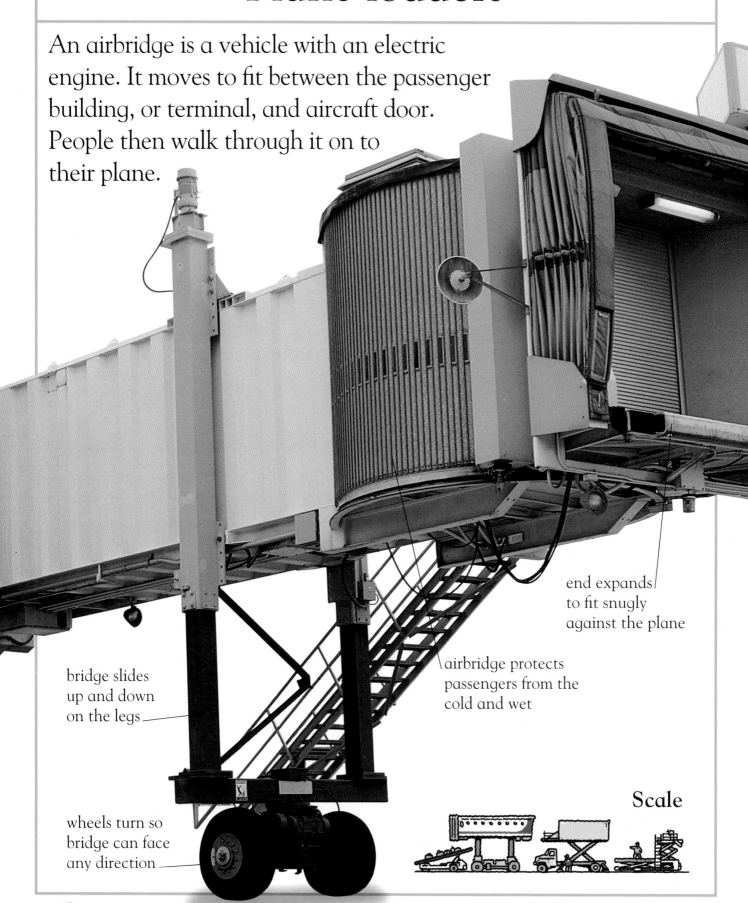

end expands to fit snugly against the plane

airbridge protects passengers from the cold and wet

bridge slides up and down on the legs

wheels turn so bridge can face any direction

Scale

Goods carried by plane are called the **cargo**. A plane's kitchen is called a **galley**.

Amazing Facts

A big jet that carries 300 people can be unloaded, cleaned, filled with fuel and supplies, then reloaded with passengers and cargo in less than one hour.

A 747 is loaded with 840 meals, 80 litres of juice, and 40 litres of water for a long distance flight.

Moving meals

Catering trucks, called high loaders, bring trolleys of food to the door of a plane. The food is then taken to the galley.

Ramp loader

The moving belt of a ramp loader carries luggage up to the hold. It is stacked inside by hand.

Freight loader

Heavy loads are piled on the rear deck of a freight loader. The deck then lifts up to bring the load to the cargo hold.

rear deck holds heavy containers

The **hold** of a plane is where the luggage and cargo is stored.

Snowplough

⬡ A snowplough can clear 70 tonnes of snow a minute – enough to make 1,750 small snowmen.

⬡ Fully stretched out, a plough's blades are nearly 5 m wide. That's as wide as five seven-year-olds lying end to end.

⬡ A standard runway is 46 m wide – as wide as four tennis courts next to one another.

Every day, thousands of planes with millions of passengers fly between international airports. Hold-ups at one airport can mean delays around the world. Planes must be able to take off in any weather. In bad snowstorms, a team of vehicles clears snow from the runways and taxiways.

Scale

Blade runner

Six snowploughs work together to push snow off the taxiways with their broad blades. The bottom of the blades are rubber.

  Planes roll along **taxiways** to get from the terminal to the runway.

snow is flung out of the funnel

Snow eaters
Snow blowers chew through piles of snow left by ploughs or on the runways. They blow the piles away.

snow is drawn in through the blades

Sweepers
Whatever the weather, it is very dangerous for rubbish to get under a plane's wheels or in its engines. Small trucks sweep up the apron all day long.

large blade cuts through debris

brush sweeps

Concorde

AMAZING FACTS

At cruising speed, Concorde flies 1.6 km in under three seconds – faster than a rifle bullet.

The fastest passenger plane is called Concorde. It flies at over 2,000 kph. This is faster than the speed that sound travels through air, so Concorde is called a "supersonic" plane.

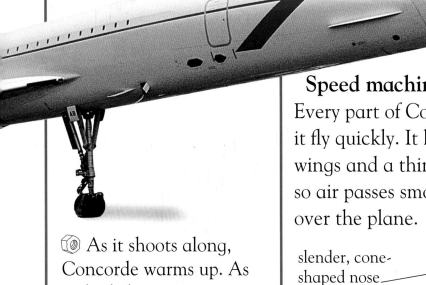

nose raised for flight

Speed machine

Every part of Concorde is designed to help it fly quickly. It has narrow, swept-back wings and a thin, sleek fuselage so air passes smoothly over the plane.

slender, cone-shaped nose

As it shoots along, Concorde warms up. As its body heats up, it gets bigger by 22 cm – nearly as long as a ruler.

Time warp

Concorde takes only four hours to fly from London to New York. That's about half the time it takes a 747 to do the same journey.

nose dropped for landing

Concorde must lower its long nose before take off and landing. Otherwise the pilot can't see over it to the runway.

Scale

Double glazing

A visor slides up over Concorde's front windows to make the shape of the nose smoother so air can flow past it more easily.

cabin has room for 100 passengers

visor

cockpit

Travel comfort

Concorde flies over 15,000 m high. This far up there are no gusty air currents to make the ride bumpy, so passengers have a smooth journey.

rudder

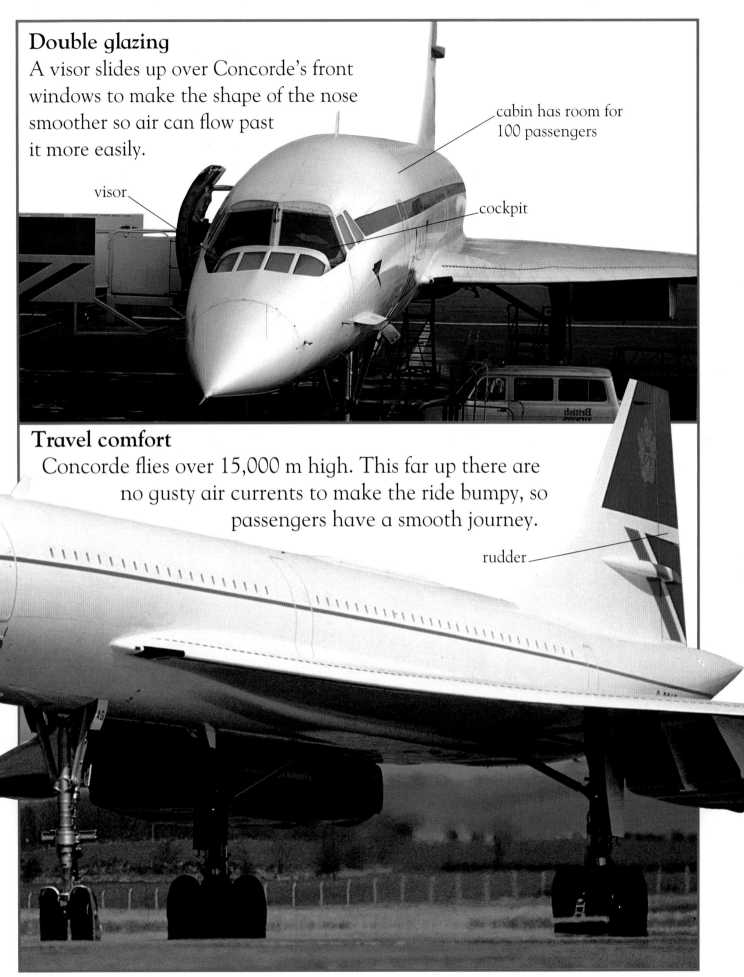

The captain and co-pilot sit in a cabin called the **cockpit**.

Airport tug

If a plane parked near an airport could reverse, the force of its engine would blow out the airport's windows. Powerful vehicles called airport tugs shove planes in or out of their parking positions.

Scale

Large tugs can pull planes that weigh eight times as much as they do. Could you lift eight of your friends?

driver's cab contains the radio controls

large mirror helps the driver see all around

low, flat body easily slides under a plane

ATL1

hook for towbar

Tugs are vehicles that push or pull other machines.

Preparing for pushback

The tug driver gets permission from ground control to move the plane, and radios the flight crew to say what is happening. They may be so high in the cockpit that they can't see the tug.

heavy weight of the tug stops it from slipping

steel bar

Mighty shove

The tug hitches a thick steel towbar from its front to the front wheel of the plane. Then it begins to crawl forwards, pushing the plane back.

front hook for towbar

nearly the whole of a tug's body contains the engine

extra-wide wheels grip the runway

Helicopter

Helicopters are very different from aeroplanes. Instead of fixed wings they have long, thin blades that spin round and round, pulling the craft straight up into the air. Helicopters can fly forwards, sideways, and backwards, and can hover (stay in one place) in the air. This helicopter is an air ambulance.

Scale

rotor whirls the blades around 500 times a minute

blade tip speed is about 725 kph

blades tilt to fly a helicopter forwards or backwards

metal skids

Landing **skids** are an alternative to wheels for some helicopters.

Fast aid

The back doors of this air ambulance are called clam-shell doors. They open to take in two patients on stretchers. In an emergency, a doctor has enough equipment to operate on the spot.

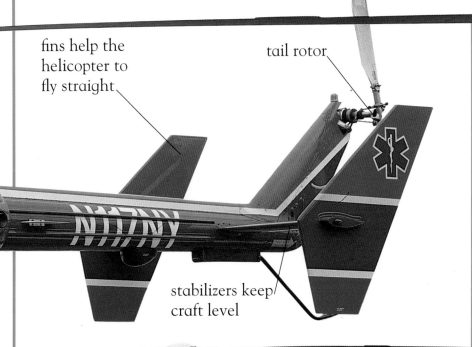

fins help the helicopter to fly straight

tail rotor

stabilizers keep craft level

⬡ The engine in an average size helicopter is about the same size as a backpack.

Good vision

Big windows allow the pilot to see what is in front and to the side of the helicopter. They have windscreen wipers, just like a car.

⬡ This helicopter's spotlight shines as brightly as 16,000 candles.

🔩 The **tail rotor** stops the helicopter from spinning around under the main rotor. 🔩